31

UP

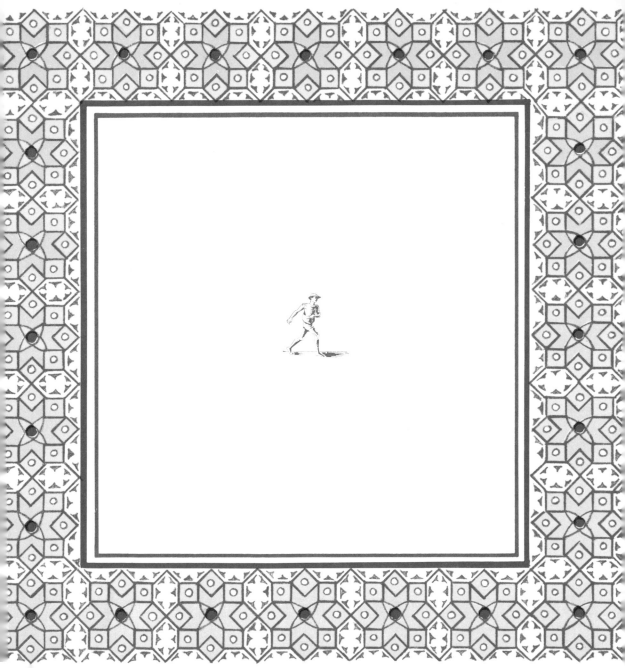

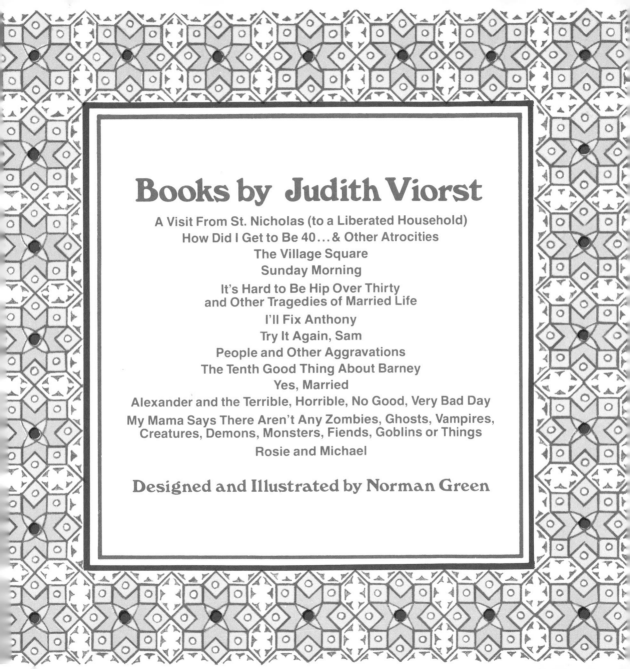

Books by Judith Viorst

Designed and Illustrated by Norman Green

A Visit From St. Nicholas

To a Liberated Household

From the original written in 1823 by Clement Clarke Moore

BY JUDITH VIORST

• Simon and Schuster • New York •

Copyright © 1976 by Judith Viorst
Illustrations Copyright © 1977 by Simon & Schuster
A Division of Gulf & Western Corporation
All rights reserved
including the right of reproduction
in whole or in part in any form
Published by Simon and Schuster
A Division of Gulf & Western Corporation
Simon & Schuster Building
Rockefeller Center
1230 Avenue of the Americas
New York, New York 10020

The author is indebted to *Redbook,* where this work
originally appeared in slightly different form.

Manufactured in the United States of America

1 2 3 4 5 6 7 8 9 10

Library of Congress Cataloging in Publication Data
Viorst, Judith.
A visit from St. Nicholas (to a liberated household).
I. Moore, Clement Clarke, 1779-1863. The night
before Christmas. II. Title.
PS3572.I6V55   811'.5'4   77-24658
ISBN 0-671-22868-4

For Sey Chassler

'Twas the night before Christmas, when All through the house

¶which, according to their marriage contract, he cleans on Mondays, Wednesdays, Fridays, and alternate Sundays and she cleans on Tuesdays, Thursdays, Saturdays, and alternate Sundays, except that on the weeks when he goes to the supermarket she has to clean an extra day, and vice versa¶

Not a creature Was stirring, Not even a mouse

¶which he has started to feel very comfortable about admitting he is terrified of, thanks to the repudiation of outmoded clichés attributing fear of rodents only to women¶.

The stockings

*they were actually *her* stockings but he wouldn't, says Joyce, have a single qualm about wearing them, for he feels secure enough in his own masculinity to no longer need to define himself through external symbols*

Were hung by
The chimney with care,
In hopes that St. Nicholas
Soon would be there.

The children

which include a girl, who plans to be President of the United States; a boy, who plans to marry the President of the United States; and a third child, who is free to select whatever sexual persuasion he/she desires

**Were nestled
All snug in their beds,
While visions of
Sugarplums danced
Through their heads.**

E PLURIBUS UNUM

SEAL OF THE PRESIDENT OF THE UNITED STATES

And Joyce in her kerchief,
And Rich in his cap

Although it could just as easily have been *Rich* in her kerchief and *Joyce* in his cap — please see earlier statement on external symbols**▶**,

Had just settled
Their brains

Awhose capacity for logic and reason and abstract thinking and reading a map of New Jersey is not, Joyce would like to observe, intrinsically greater in males than it is in females**▶**

For a long winter's nap,

When out on the lawn

❦ which presents something of a problem because, although he loves to mow it and she hates to, they both agree that it wouldn't be good for the children to see their parents in stereotypical roles, so *she* mows it ❦

There arose such a clatter,
She sprang
From the bed to see
What was the matter

❦ for, having earned a black belt in karate, Joyce now does the springing out of bed, dispelling the myth that a family's physical safety always has to be in the charge of the man and also dispelling the myth that a woman is somehow less of a "woman" — whatever *that* means — just because she breaks boards with a blow of her hand ❦.

Away to the window
She flew like a flash,
Tore open the shutters
And threw up the sash.

The moon on the chest
Of the new-fallen snow

I actually, it's *breast* of the new-fallen snow, but Joyce
deplores this usage of breast, along with such sexist
metaphors as Mother Nature, Father Time, and Manhattan

Gave the luster of midday
To objects below,

When, what to her
Wondering eyes
Should appear,
But a miniature sleigh,
And eight tiny reindeer,
With a little old driver
So lively and quick,
She knew in a moment
It must be St. Nick

(although Joyce would like it made perfectly clear that the reason she knew in a moment it must be St. Nick had nothing whatsoever to do with the attribution of liveliness and quickness — as distinct, say, from passivity — to a member of the masculine persuasion).

More rapid than eagles
His coursers they came,
And he whistled,
And shouted,
And called them by name:

"Now, Dasher! now, Dancer! Now, Prancer and Vixen! On, Comet! on, Cupid! On, Donder and Blitzen!

Joyce points out that there appears to be an equitable distribution of male and female reindeer, with six nonsexist names—Dasher, Dancer, Prancer, Comet, Donder, and Blitzen; one indisputably feminine name—Vixen; and one name, Cupid, which classically is masculine. Although she is gratified, she says, by this evidence of equal employment opportunities, she nonetheless senses something invidious in the fact that while the male name, Cupid, refers to the god of love, the female name, Vixen, is defined by the dictionary as "an ill-tempered or quarrelsome woman."

DANCER

DASHER

VIXEN

PRANCER

To the top of the porch!
To the top of the wall!
Now dash away!
Dash away!
Dash away, all!"

As dry leaves that before
The wild hurricane fly,
When they meet
With an obstacle,
Mount to the sky,

So up to the housetop
The coursers they flew,
With the sleigh
Full of toys

which, needless to say, were selected without any reference to outdated notions of gender "appropriateness," for today, Joyce reminds us, every girl can choose to be a doctor, a jockey, an astronaut, or a boy,

And St. Nicholas too.

And then, in a twinkling,
She heard on the roof
The prancing and pawing
Of each little hoof.
As she drew in her head,
And was turning around,
Down the chimney
St. Nicholas came
With a bound

A showy gymnastic performance which was certainly not required, Joyce notes, to get down the chimney, and thus can be accounted for only in terms of macho exhibitionism.

He was dressed all in fur

about which, says Joyce, she finds herself of two minds, for while she has to respect a man who believes that things like furs and jewels and perfume ought to be worn not only by females but males, she nonetheless fears that any man who would wear on his back the pelt of our vanishing wildlife is capable of conducting himself with equal insensitivity and callousness to other oppressed minorities, such as women

From his head to his foot, And his clothes Were all tarnished with Ashes and soot

the washing out of which, Joyce fervently hopes, won't be left to poor *Mrs.* St. Nick, who, she feels, should stop living in the shadow of her husband and develop her own identity.

A bundle of toys he had
Flung on his back,
And he looked like a peddler
Just opening his pack.
His eyes-how they twinkled!
His dimples, how merry!
His cheeks were like roses,
His nose like a cherry!

His droll little mouth
Was drawn up like a bow,
And the beard of his chin
Was as white as the snow

Joyce feels that she ought to point out that while a *man* who has a beard as white as the snow can look not only distinguished but also sexy, a woman is forced to use bleaches and dyes in order to not be regarded as over the hill because, she continues pointing out, our chauvinistic society tends to see women as objects instead of people.

The stump of a pipe

❡which, Joyce points out, she too is entitled to smoke—
not only under state and federal law but also, if ERA
passes, the Constitution❡

He held tight in his teeth,
And the smoke it encircled
His head like a wreath.
He had a wide face

❡actually, the face is described as *broad,* a word which
in other contexts, Joyce observes, is exceedingly derogatory
to women and ought, whenever possible, to be extirpated❡

And a round little belly
That shook when he laughed,
Like a bowlful of jelly.

He was chubby and plump

in spite of which, Joyce feels that she ought to point out, a man can look distinguished and also sexy, while a woman who is "chubby and plump," and furthermore has — see above — a "round little belly," is frequently regarded as unattractive, because, she continues pointing out, our chauvinistic society tends to judge women by girlie-magazine standards,

A right jolly old elf,
And she laughed
When she saw him
In spite of herself.

love
Santa

A wink of his eye

¶ which is certainly not the deceptively innocent act, Joyce says, that it seems to be, but represents — unconsciously, of course — a sexual assault¶.

And a twist of his head
Soon gave her to know
She had nothing to dread

¶ though if she *did* have something to dread — see statement above on unconscious meaning of wink — Joyce is very sure *she* wouldn't dread it — see earlier statement on black belt in karate¶.

He spoke not a word,
But went straight
To his work

¶ which Joyce considers no more *his* work than *her* work, arguing that the job requirements surely could be met by anyone of either sex who can steer reindeer, fit through chimneys, and get along well with elves ¶,

And filled all the stockings,
Then turned with a jerk,
And laying his finger
Aside of his nose,
And giving a nod,
Up the chimney he rose.

He sprang to his sleigh,
To his team gave a whistle

the sexual implications of which, Joyce observes, are similar to those discussed under wink, especially when the whistle is directed, not at reindeer, but at women,

And away they all flew
Like the down of a thistle.
But she heard him exclaim,
Ere he drove out of sight,
"Happy Christmas to all

and by "all," Joyce says, she hopes he means not women and men but independent persons, persons defined by their interests, their work, their character, and their minds but not — perish the thought! — by their anatomy

And to all a good night!"